# First World War
## and Army of Occupation
# War Diary
## France, Belgium and Germany

3 CAVALRY DIVISION
6 Cavalry Brigade
'C' Battery Royal Horse Artillery
22 March 1915 - 30 November 1918

WO95/1152/2

The Naval & Military Press Ltd
www.nmarchive.com
**Published in association with The National Archives**

Published by

## The Naval & Military Press Ltd

Unit 10 Ridgewood Industrial Park,

Uckfield, East Sussex,

TN22 5QE England

Tel: +44 (0) 1825 749494

www.naval-military-press.com

www.nmarchive.com

*This diary has been reprinted in facsimile from the original. Any imperfections are inevitably reproduced and the quality may fall short of modern type and cartographic standards.*

**© Crown Copyright**
**Images reproduced by permission of The National Archives, London, England, 2015.**

# Contents

| Document type | Place/Title | Date From | Date To |
|---|---|---|---|
| Heading | WO95/1152/2 3 Cavalry Division 6 Cavalry Brigade "C" Battery Royal Horse Artillery Mar 1915-Nov 1918 | | |
| Heading | 1915-1918 3rd Cavalry Division 6th Cavalry Brigade."C" Battery R.H.A. Mar 1915-Nov 1918 | | |
| Heading | 3rd Cav. Div "C" Batty R.H.A. 22nd March-Dec 1915 Nov 1918 Vol. I | | |
| War Diary | Kemmel Belgium | 22/03/1915 | 02/06/1915 |
| War Diary | Boeseghem France | 03/06/1915 | 20/06/1915 |
| War Diary | Flechin France | 06/08/1915 | 30/08/1915 |
| War Diary | Hinges | 03/09/1915 | 16/09/1915 |
| War Diary | Flechin | 16/09/1915 | 20/09/1915 |
| War Diary | Bois Des Dames | 20/09/1915 | 24/09/1915 |
| War Diary | Corons de Rutoire | 25/09/1915 | 26/09/1915 |
| War Diary | Fosse No 7 de Bethune | 27/09/1915 | 29/09/1915 |
| War Diary | Bois De Dames | 30/09/1915 | 02/10/1915 |
| War Diary | Cauchy A La Tour | 03/10/1915 | 19/10/1915 |
| War Diary | Laires | 21/10/1915 | 29/10/1915 |
| War Diary | Sains Les Fressins | 07/11/1915 | 28/12/1915 |
| Heading | 3c 6" Bty R H A Jan 1916 Vol II | | |
| War Diary | Sains Les Fressin | 01/01/1916 | 04/01/1916 |
| War Diary | Estree Blanche | 06/01/1916 | 07/01/1916 |
| War Diary | Labourse Vermelles | 08/01/1916 | 08/01/1916 |
| War Diary | Vermelles | 09/01/1916 | 23/02/1916 |
| War Diary | Sains Les Fressin | 23/02/1916 | 31/07/1916 |
| War Diary | La Neuville | 01/08/1916 | 01/08/1916 |
| War Diary | Soues | 02/08/1916 | 02/08/1916 |
| War Diary | Neuf Moulin | 04/08/1916 | 04/08/1916 |
| War Diary | Grand Preaux | 05/08/1916 | 05/08/1916 |
| War Diary | Wambercourt | 05/08/1916 | 10/09/1916 |
| War Diary | Dominois | 11/09/1916 | 11/09/1916 |
| War Diary | Drucat | 12/09/1916 | 12/09/1916 |
| War Diary | La Chaussee | 13/09/1916 | 14/09/1916 |
| War Diary | Bussy | 15/09/1916 | 17/09/1916 |
| War Diary | Querrieu | 17/09/1916 | 22/09/1916 |
| War Diary | Soues | 23/09/1916 | 23/09/1916 |
| War Diary | Bealcourt | 24/09/1916 | 24/09/1916 |
| War Diary | Douriez | 25/09/1916 | 30/09/1916 |
| War Diary | Mesnil | 01/11/1916 | 20/11/1916 |
| War Diary | Aveluy Marieux | 21/11/1916 | 21/11/1916 |
| War Diary | Bertaucourt | 22/11/1916 | 22/11/1916 |
| War Diary | St Riquier | 23/11/1916 | 23/11/1916 |
| War Diary | Roussent | 24/11/1916 | 15/12/1916 |
| War Diary | Renty | 16/12/1916 | 16/12/1916 |
| War Diary | Aire | 17/12/1916 | 04/03/1917 |
| War Diary | Dennebroeucq | 05/03/1917 | 05/03/1917 |
| War Diary | | 06/03/1917 | 31/03/1917 |
| War Diary | Lespinoy | 01/04/1917 | 04/04/1917 |
| War Diary | Contes | 05/04/1917 | 06/04/1917 |
| War Diary | Verquerie le Bourq | 07/04/1917 | 07/04/1917 |
| War Diary | Fosseux | 08/04/1917 | 08/04/1917 |

| | | | |
|---|---|---|---|
| War Diary | Arras | 09/04/1917 | 11/04/1917 |
| War Diary | Fosseaux | 12/04/1917 | 15/04/1917 |
| War Diary | Boufflers | 16/04/1917 | 18/04/1917 |
| War Diary | Roussent | 19/04/1917 | 30/04/1917 |
| Miscellaneous | Supplimentary War Diary Map Regiment Sheet 51 B 1/40,000. | | |
| War Diary | Roussent | 01/05/1917 | 11/05/1917 |
| War Diary | Tortefontaine | 12/05/1917 | 12/05/1917 |
| War Diary | Outrebois | 13/05/1917 | 13/05/1917 |
| War Diary | Havernas | 14/05/1917 | 14/05/1917 |
| War Diary | Bussy Les Daours | 15/05/1917 | 15/05/1917 |
| War Diary | Harbonniere | 16/05/1917 | 16/05/1917 |
| War Diary | Roisel | 17/05/1917 | 31/05/1917 |
| War Diary | Ronsoy | 01/06/1917 | 04/06/1917 |
| War Diary | Roisel | 05/06/1917 | 05/06/1917 |
| War Diary | Buire | 05/06/1917 | 09/06/1917 |
| War Diary | Ronsoy Buire | 10/06/1917 | 10/06/1917 |
| War Diary | Buire Epehy | 10/06/1917 | 30/06/1917 |
| War Diary | Epehy | 01/07/1917 | 07/07/1917 |
| War Diary | Roisel | 07/07/1917 | 10/07/1917 |
| War Diary | Bray | 11/07/1917 | 11/07/1917 |
| War Diary | Sarton | 12/07/1917 | 12/07/1917 |
| War Diary | Letree Wamin | 13/07/1917 | 13/07/1917 |
| War Diary | Hernicourt | 14/07/1917 | 14/07/1917 |
| War Diary | Auchel | 15/07/1917 | 15/07/1917 |
| War Diary | La Motte Baudet | 16/07/1917 | 31/08/1917 |
| War Diary | St Omer | 01/09/1917 | 01/09/1917 |
| War Diary | St Momelin | 02/09/1917 | 02/09/1917 |
| War Diary | Herzeele | 06/09/1917 | 31/10/1917 |
| War Diary | Dailymail Wood Near Baulincourt | 01/08/1918 | 31/08/1918 |
| War Diary | Pt Bouret | 01/09/1918 | 05/09/1918 |
| War Diary | Presnoy | 06/09/1918 | 20/09/1918 |
| War Diary | Fortel | 21/09/1918 | 31/10/1918 |
| War Diary | Equancourt | 01/11/1918 | 12/11/1918 |
| War Diary | Wasmes | 13/11/1918 | 24/11/1918 |
| War Diary | Warisoulx | 25/11/1918 | 30/11/1918 |

(2)

WO 95/1152

3 Cavalry Division
6 Cavalry Brigade
'C' Battery Royal Horse Artillery

Mar 1915 - Nov 1918

1915-1918
3RD CAVALRY DIVISION
6TH CAVALRY BRIGADE.

'C' BATTERY R.H.A.
MAR 1915-NOV 1918.

9/10 Cav. Bde

"C" Batt: R.H.A.
22nd November — Dec
1915
Nov 1918      Vol. I

121/7930

Army Form C. 2118.

# WAR DIARY
## or
## INTELLIGENCE SUMMARY.
*(Erase heading not required.)*

| Place | Date | Hour | Summary of Events and Information | Remarks and references to Appendices |
|---|---|---|---|---|
| Maynard Aetjaen | March 22nd 1915 | | Battery marched from Walloon Cappel to Kemmel and went into action near the Chateau North of Kemmel village – The Battery remained in action until June 3rd 1915 | PETIT BOIS |
| | 28– | | Battery was ordered to cover the German trenches about | PETIT BOIS |
| | | | a zone of about 8 degrees– | |
| | 23–31st | | The Battery was very busy, the duty being the artillery fire on either side beyond registration | |
| | 1st April | | An alternative position was selected for the Battery, should a retirement become necessary – The gun pits were dug on the 5th April – | |
| | 14th & 15th | | Nothing particular to record that times Brush finally fired upon Sen: MEDELSTEDT FARM & PECKHAM FARM. 1E a line of Trenches from W. of WYTSCHAETE | |
| | 17th April | | The 5th Division (North of us) were ordered to attack Hill 60 at 7pm. The Battery Cooperated by firing about 70 rounds between 7.45pm and 8.10 pm – There was very little retaliation | |
| | 18th–22nd | | Nothing to record | |
| | 19th April | | Lieutenant M. W. NUISH left the Battery & Joined the Royal Flying Corps – | |

Army Form C. 2118.

# WAR DIARY
## or
## INTELLIGENCE SUMMARY.
(Erase heading not required.)

Instructions regarding War Diaries and Intelligence Summaries are contained in F. S. Regs., Part II. and the Staff Manual respectively. Title pages will be prepared in manuscript.

| Place | Date | Hour | Summary of Events and Information | Remarks and references to Appendices |
|---|---|---|---|---|
| KEMMEL BELGIUM | 21st April | | Lieutenant H.E. CHAPMAN joined the Battery from R.H.A. Amesbury Plain. 3rd Cavalry Division. | |
| | 22nd April | | Heavy firing was heard N. of Ypres. | |
| | 23rd April | | German shells the front line North of Ypres, having attacked with gas. Battery was harnessed to be ready in case of an attack. | |
| | 24 & 25 | | Nothing to record | |
| | 27th April | | We blew up a mine under the German Trenches near PETIT BOIS. Battery harnessed to cooperate if necessary. | |
| | 28th April | | Battery has orders to reconnoitre a position East of NEUVE EGLISE. This position was occupied on the 2nd May. | |
| | 7th May | | The battery shot successfully at a Zeppelin trench near MAEDELSTEDE FARM. | |
| | 10th May | | We exploded a mine under the German trenches at PECKHAM FARM. The battery cooperated with it's fire. | |

1577 Wt.W10791/1773 500,000 1/15 D. D. & L. A.D.S.S./Forms/C. 2118.

# WAR DIARY
## or
## INTELLIGENCE SUMMARY.
(Erase heading not required.)

Army Form C. 2118.

Instructions regarding War Diaries and Intelligence Summaries are contained in F. S. Regs., Part II. and the Staff Manual respectively. Title pages will be prepared in manuscript.

| Place | Date | Hour | Summary of Events and Information | Remarks and references to Appendices |
|---|---|---|---|---|
| KEMMEL BELGIUM | 16th May | | At 7.30pm the battery fired on PECKHAM FARM in support of a French mortar. | |
| | 17th May | | At 4.30pm a Zeppelin airship apparently damaged was seen flying East over ZONNEBEKE. | |
| | 20th May | | Battery fired incendiary shells experimentally, at WYTSCHAETE. These shells appear to be of very little value. | |
| | 28th May | | Infantry reported snipers in farmhouse in PECKHAM FARM and asked for artillery fire to be brought to bear at this point. The battery effectually shelled the snipers. Scarcely any shells were fired at PETIT BOIS without visible results. | |
| | 29th May | | Battery drew several respirators as a protection against asphyxiating gases, and has its first respirator parade. | |

Army Form C. 2118.

# WAR DIARY
## or
## INTELLIGENCE SUMMARY.
(Erase heading not required.)

Instructions regarding War Diaries and Intelligence Summaries are contained in F.S. Regs., Part II. and the Staff Manual respectively. Title pages will be prepared in manuscript.

| Place | Date | Hour | Summary of Events and Information | Remarks and references to Appendices |
|---|---|---|---|---|
| KEMMEL BELGIUM | 1st June | | Battery received orders that I would be relieved | |
| " | 2nd June | | At 8pm the guns were withdrawn to hopes live billets near LOCRE - | |
| BOESEGHEM, Boesinghem FRANCE | June 3 | | Battery marched to billets at Boesinghem - BOESEGHEM. | |
| " | 5th June | | The 6th Cavalry brigade came back from Ypres and the battery became again attd. rejoined it - | |
| | 14th June | | The Mobile Section R.H.A. Ammunition Column joined the battery commanded by LIEUTENANT R. PATRICK. (Special reserve R.F.A.) | |
| | 18th June | | The Commander in Chief FIELD MARSHAL SIR JOHN FRENCH inspected and spoke to 6th Cavalry brigade at STEENBECQUE | |
| | 19th June | | Whilst the battery here instructions the French hotels which hotels The bomb inside the fuel proton exploded slightly wounding Brig Genl D. Campbell and M.S. Wheeler DAVIES | |

**Army Form C. 2118.**

# WAR DIARY
## or
## INTELLIGENCE SUMMARY.
*(Erase heading not required.)*

Instructions regarding War Diaries and Intelligence Summaries are contained in F. S. Regs., Part II. and the Staff Manual respectively. Title pages will be prepared in manuscript.

| Place | Date | Hour | Summary of Events and Information | Remarks and references to Appendices |
|---|---|---|---|---|
| Buseghem. France. | 8th August. | 8am. | First contingent of A/175 Siege Artr. arrived for the Battery — | |
| Flechin France | 8th August. | | The battery moved to Flechin | |
| | 12th August. | | Major. J.W.F. LAMONT. R.F.A. left the Battery to command the 30th Brigade R.F.A. | |
| | 13th August. | | The battery had a party under Lieut. MANN R.F.A. to dig gun pits & shelters at ARMENTIERES | |
| | 16th August. | | B.S.M. TOTT and Serjt. BILLING left the Battery on becoming Commissioned | |
| | 29th August. | | CAPTAIN R.C.F. MAITLAND R.H.A. joined the Battery to command it from R. Battery R.H.A. | |
| | 29th August. | | Orders to be ready to move on 30th August & join the 1st Army. | |
| | 30th August. | | The unit was put off until Sept 3rd | |
| Hinges | 3rd September. | | The Battery marched from Flechin at 2 pm via Lillers to HINGES arriving in billets after dark, and joined the 7th Army. | |
| " | 4th September. | | Under orders of 7th Divisional Artillery. The Battery was allotted a position at VERMELLES, and ordered to dig pits for the guns — a gun position at | |

Army Form C. 2118.

# WAR DIARY
## or
## INTELLIGENCE SUMMARY.
*(Erase heading not required.)*

Instructions regarding War Diaries and Intelligence Summaries are contained in F.S. Regs., Part II. and the Staff Manual respectively. Title pages will be prepared in manuscript.

| Place | Date | Hour | Summary of Events and Information | Remarks and references to Appendices |
|---|---|---|---|---|
| HINGES | 5th September | | Gun position at VERMELLES reconnoitred, and a party of men started work on the post at night. | |
| " | 6th | " | Zone of fire allotted to battery from a bearing 60° True North to 110° True North. The targets included front of the enemy's front line trench and point C.C.P. 229 behind it. | |
| " | 7th | " | Party digging at VERMELLES. | |
| " | 8th | " | Ordered to stop digging at VERMELLES and to carry on experiments with High Explosive shell. | |
| " | 9th | " | Carry out experiments that the Experienced hill to be reconnoitred at VERMELLES. Battery had orders that digging was to and that digging was started at VERMELLES. | |
| " | 10th | " | Digging again started at VERMELLES. | |
| " | 11th | " | Orders to stop digging at VERMELLES Battery to proceed to MEERUT Division on 12th to carry out experiments with 750 rounds of High Explosive Shell. | |
| " | 12th | " | Battery Commander and Battery Staff and Captain with billeting party sent to LA GORGUE to headquarters MEERUT DIVISIONAL ARTILLERY, Battery allotted gun position at PONT DU HEM from S. of LA BASSÉE ROAD. Camping Camp – Cancelled. Experimental practice with H.E. shell at 3 am orders came – cancelling Experimental practice with H.E. shell returned HINGES. | |

157 Wt-W.0791/1713 500,000 1/15 D. D & L Ltd. A.D.S.S./Forms/C. 2118.

# WAR DIARY
## or
## INTELLIGENCE SUMMARY.

(Erase heading not required.)

Army Form C. 2118.

Instructions regarding War Diaries and Intelligence Summaries are contained in F. S. Regs., Part II. and the Staff Manual respectively. Title pages will be prepared in manuscript.

| Place | Date | Hour | Summary of Events and Information | Remarks and references to Appendices |
|---|---|---|---|---|
| HINGES | 13th | P/Tel | Orders received to reconnoitre trenches from position at VERMELLES - Party sent up under Lieuts CHAPMAN & BOYKAZ. Corporal MELLUM wounded by a premature burst from a 60 pr. while digging at VERMELLES | |
| " | 14th | " | Digging from position at VERMELLES | |
| " | 15th | " | Orders received to rejoin the 8th Cavalry Brigade on the following day | |
| " | 16th | " | Marched at 1 pm via CHOCQUES and LILLERS to FLECHIN Occupied original billets | |
| FLECHIN | 17th | " | Nothing to record. | |
| | 18th | " | " " " | |
| | 19th | " | Orders to be ready & move on the following day with 3 days rations - for men and forage for horses - | |
| | 20th | " | Left FLECHIN at 4.30pm for rendezvous with 6th Cavalry Brigade at BELLERY at 6.30pm, marched via BUCHET & BOIS des DAMES | |

# WAR DIARY
## INTELLIGENCE SUMMARY

Army Form C. 2118.

| Place | Date | Hour | Summary of Events and Information | Remarks and references to Appendices |
|---|---|---|---|---|
| Bois des DAMES | 20th Sept. | | BIVOUACKED in Bois des DAMES, having arrived there at 11.30pm | |
| " | 21st Sept. | | Moved to a more comfortable place in Bois des DAMES. | |
| " | 22nd | | 1 Officer went to reconnoitre roads from NOEUX les MINES towards German lines — first line trenches | |
| " | 23rd | | 2 Officers went to reconnoitre roads from NOEUX les MINES towards German first line trenches | |
| " | 24th | | Orders to be prepared to move at short notice — further orders to be ready. Moved at 5.30 pm on the following day — H.Q. | |
| CORONS de RUTOIRE | 25th | | Moved to employ our PLACE de BRUAY at 7am — The brigade marched at 5.30pm to VAUDRICOURT — Halted at VAUDRICOURT 1½ hours, the 8th Cavalry brigade marched to CORONS de RUTOIRE the battery being billeted up to the 3 sections for this march one section being sent beyond — CORONS de RUTOIRE. The battery remained for the rest of the day at CORONS de RUTOIRE. The 6th Cavalry brigade had received orders to form an L to the DOUVE CANAL but these orders were cancelled as there was no gap — At 6.30pm battery had orders to bivouac for the night at CORONS de RUTOIRE | |

# WAR DIARY or INTELLIGENCE SUMMARY

Army Form C. 2118.

| Place | Date | Hour | Summary of Events and Information | Remarks and references to Appendices |
|---|---|---|---|---|
| Corons de Rutoire | 26th | September | Battery was ordered into action to prepare a portion just S. of FOSSE No 3, and to be able to cover the MAROC ridge — at 12 o'c. Mid-day — at 2 pm Battery was ordered into action in this position to barrage ammo dump at Cité St ELIE — The Battery fired 40 rounds of Shrapnel — Received in action orders of 15th Divisional artillery during the night to act as fire. | |
| Fosse No 7 de BETHUNE | 27th | " | Battery brought forward to a position just E. of FOSSE No 7 during Watering without live German trenches, orders to be ready to cooperate with the Infantry attack on Hill 70, and to have an area of about 40 km in front. Battery was not to fire on any RUIT 14 Bis — Further orders came — Further orders Gunner HARVEY slightly wounded — Accent. | |
| " | 28th | " | 9.45 pm orders to barrage with H.E. 25 rounds an hour between HULLUCH and PUIT 14 Bis | |
| " | 29th | " | 2 am Orders received to cease barrage at 5 am and withdraw at 5.30 am — Battery to rejoin 6th Cavalry Brigade at NOEUX les MINES — arrived at Bois des DAMES at 11 am and horses — Thir — | |

**Army Form C. 2118.**

# WAR DIARY
## or
## INTELLIGENCE SUMMARY.
*(Erase heading not required.)*

Instructions regarding War Diaries and Intelligence Summaries are contained in F. S. Regs., Part II. and the Staff Manual respectively. Title pages will be prepared in manuscript.

| Place | Date | Hour | Summary of Events and Information | Remarks and references to Appendices |
|---|---|---|---|---|
| Bois du Ammes | 30th Sept. | | ⎱ Bivouacks in Bois du Ammes. Nothing to record ⎰ | |
| | 1st Oct. | | | |
| | 2nd Oct. | | | |
| Cauchy a la Tour | 3rd Oct. | | 9th Cavalry Brigade moved back, the Battery moves to Cauchy a la Tour to billets | |
| " | 4 | | | |
| | 5 | | | |
| | 6 | | | |
| | 7 | | | |
| | 8 | | | |
| | 9 | | | |
| | 10 | | | |
| | 11 | | | |
| | 12 | | | |
| | 13 | | | |

**Army Form C. 2118.**

# WAR DIARY
## or
## INTELLIGENCE SUMMARY.
*(Erase heading not required.)*

Instructions regarding War Diaries and Intelligence Summaries are contained in F.S. Regs., Part II. and the Staff Manual respectively. Title pages will be prepared in manuscript.

| Place | Date | Hour | Summary of Events and Information | Remarks and references to Appendices |
|---|---|---|---|---|
| COUCHY à la Tour | Oct 19th | | 6 Cavalry moved further west. The Battery billetted at Febvin PALFART | |
| LAIRES | 21st | | Brigade moved into "permanent"(?) winter quarters at LAIRES. Battery " " " " | |
| | 23rd | | Capt Nunn posted to Home Establishment & departs to England. | |
| | 24th 28th 29th | | Capt MAITLAND " " " 2nd Lieut H.R. BENNETT joined the Battery as fourth Subaltern. Major A.E. ERSKINE took over command of the Battery. All horses under cover. Good accommodation. Water supply fair – probably rare in summer. 21 horse cast, mostly as unsuitable for R.H.A. | |
| | Nov 7th | | 21 remounts arrived. Good lot on the whole. | |
| Mr. | Nov 17 | | Whole Cavalry Brigade moved further WEST. Battery moved to SAINS LES FRESSINS about 8 miles SW of FRUGES. | |

Army Form C. 2118.

# WAR DIARY
## or
## INTELLIGENCE SUMMARY.
(Erase heading not required.)

| Place | Date | Hour | Summary of Events and Information | Remarks and references to Appendices |
|---|---|---|---|---|
| SAINS LES FRESSINS | November 1915 17 Nov | (cont) | Good billets. All horses under cover. Water supply known for. Only hards to water from. In summer probably water would be scarce. | a_ |
| | 18th do | | Battery settled down to rubbing up drill, training young NCO's and telephonists. Owing to the Battery being on a side road and owing to the hilly country, motor lorries do not now deliver rations & forage to the Battery. Have to send for rations & forage to CREQUY. | a_ |

**Army Form C. 2118**

# WAR DIARY
## or
## INTELLIGENCE SUMMARY
*(Erase heading not required.)*

Instructions regarding War Diaries and Intelligence Summaries are contained in F.S. Regs., Part II. and the Staff Manual respectively. Title Pages will be prepared in manuscript.

| Place | Date | Hour | Summary of Events and Information | Remarks and references to Appendices |
|---|---|---|---|---|
| Sainneles | Dec 1st 1915 | | | |
| Fresnes | Dec 8th | | | |
| | Dec 18 | | 24 Horses & Battery cart, mostly as remounts for R.H.A. | |
| | | | 24 Remounts arrived from Bordeaux for Battery — mostly English horses, a few American. | |
| | Dec 25 | | A cheery Xmas day. Inhabitants of village did men well, giving them the use of their rooms, fires, cooking etc. Officers played in a hockey match during the afternoon at Bryan Head Quarters. | |
| | Dec 28 | | Orders received to prepare for a move. | |

Phillies
Major
C.C.Div. OSA

"C. Sty. R.A.A
Jan 1916.
Vol II

"C" Battery RHA   Vol 1   1916   Page 1

# WAR DIARY or INTELLIGENCE SUMMARY

Army Form C. 2118

| Place | Date | Hour | Summary of Events and Information | Remarks and references to Appendices |
|---|---|---|---|---|
| SAINS LES FRESSIN | 1/1/16 | | Battery left billets at 9 am & made a raining march to ESTRÉE BLANCHE arrived 1.45 pm - 17 miles. Horses stand on lines in the open. G. & 1.K. Batteries billet in the town. Forage at positions for guns. | |
| ESTRÉE BLANCHE | 4/1/16 | | Major Bailie motored to VERMELLES to look at (Field Artillery) commanded by left Section. Moved a section of 12 pdrs (Horsed Field Artillery) go on in 2 cars. Major Cooks (HAC). Major Eshine & 1st Lt Chapman go on in 2 cars - 21 miles | |
|  | 6/1/16 | | Remainder of Battery marches to La BOURSE (9 am - 2.30 pm) that night Centre Section went into action at VERMELLES Our lines which was in a Started shelling Stations for hours 2 taught its up. Piper bed. Dirty condition. Trans. for horses good. Lub. lines billets bad. | |
| LA BOURSE VERMELLES | 8/1/16 | | L.Bde RHA zone from BIG. WILLIE TRENCH to HAIRPIN CRATERS (exclusive). Battery Zone from HAIRPIN CRATERS (inclusive) to G.5 d.5.9. Batteries lines to OP (at G10 a 1.2.5) Off HULLUCH ALLEY) on line in GORDAN ALLEY. Duplicate telephone lines from OP to Bty via HULLUCH ALLEY, second line via GORDAN ALLEY. Telephone lines from OP to Bty Batt: Hd 2nd via HULLUCH ALLEY and GORDAN ALLEY. One liaison Offr in for the Brigade with one telephonist at Batt: Headquarters Battery position a good one at G.8.C.7.10, with a run of horses 300 yards in front which conceals hides horses. A few cellars for men to live in, but half the men sleep with the guns. Ammunition can be brought up to Battery position by wagons by day & night. "C" & "K" Batteries to immediate North of Battery. Spent day registering zone. | Trench map 36c N.W.3  1/10,000 |

# WAR DIARY or INTELLIGENCE SUMMARY

Army Form C. 2118

Vol I  1916  Page 2

| Place | Date | Hour | Summary of Events and Information | Remarks and references to Appendices |
|---|---|---|---|---|
| VERMELLES | 9th Jan | | Hostile fire very little. Continued to register guns. Rifle communication trenches at night under fire. | |
| | 10th Jan | | Lieut CHAPMAN took up a position with No 1 gun at G.15 d.5.8 with a view to bringing fire to bear on BIG. WILLIE. The position is fairly well covered from view, just from flashes, but is a little too close to LE RUTOIRE to be pleasant. LE RUTOIRE heavily shelled during the afternoon. | |
| | 11th Jan | | Found gun registered BIG WILLIE and the DUMP. Our front trenches in Battery zone quite quiet except for snipers from the CRATERS and the DUMP. three trenches near the DUMP however always worried by trench mortars & rifle grenades. | |
| | 12th Jan | | LE RUTOIRE heavily shelled between 9 A.M. – 11.30 A.M. "Heavies" shelled the craters pretty successfully, Battery took the opportunity of testing the machine gun in the top Tboyt. Captain E. H. MANN awarded the military cross, about N68A2M3. W Hickson the D.C.M. Daily allowance of ammunition 125 Shrapnel. NO H.E. allowed to be fired. | |
| | 13th Jan | | | |
| | 14th Jan | | Except for a certain amount of shelling on communication trenches very little hostile fire. Trench mortars very active, so Colonel Burke (Commanding 3rd D.C's) & arranged to open fire with Howard gun and a section of Battery every time mortars fired. This was most effective. Lieut CHAPMAN got his second Howard gun into position at G.16 c 5.6 with a view to firing on CRATERS + BIG WILLIE. | |
| | 15th Jan | | No 2 Howard gun registered BIG. WILLIE. | |
| | 16th Jan | | Good deal of hostile fire all day on Commn trenches. Battery retaliated. | |
| | 17th Jan | | Very clear day. VERMELLES + LE RUTOIRE shelled. | |

# WAR DIARY or INTELLIGENCE SUMMARY

Army Form C. 2118

Vol 1 1916  Page 3.

| Place | Date | Hour | Summary of Events and Information | Remarks and references to Appendices |
|---|---|---|---|---|
| Vermelles | 18th Jan | | A sniper in afternoon cattle truck at certainly edge of dump dealt with by forward gun. Forward gun fired all night at BIG WILLIE to keep trench mortar quiet. | |
| | 19th Jan | do | At 10 A.M. a hostile mine was exploded in HOHENZOLLERN redoubt in the run trench. Water Tower at Vermelles bombarded, as trees had fortunately been cut down yesterday in front of it to clear the view from it. | |
| | 20 Jan | do | Water tower in VERMELLES again shelled – Battery retaliates in HAISNES. LE RUTOIRE again shelled by small by. | |
| | 21 Jan | do | A good deal of hostile fire on Comm? trenches, with a considerable number of shrouds. Water Town again shelled. Forward gun shelled BIG WILLIE. | |
| | 22 Jan | do | Battery sniped from German trenches at eleven & again at dusk. Vermelles again shelled. Howitzers retaliates on HAISNES. | |
| | 22 Jan | do | We blew up a small mine in German trenches in trench fire of HOHENZOLLERN Redoubt. Forward gun fired on crater during the day. Forward gun shelled in afternoon. Dummy sniper of 23rd/24th Battery fired on roads behind HAISNES + CITE ST ELIE. | |
| | 24 Jan | do | Good many shells but over forward gun. | |
| | 25 Jan | do | German aeroplane very active. Front line trenches shelled pretty heavily, evidently to make us bury our printing when aeroplane was up. Battery retaliates with "G". Battery, as soon as aeroplane went down. Forward gun did good work in German crater. | |

# WAR DIARY or INTELLIGENCE SUMMARY

Vol I 1916 — Page 4

| Place | Date | Hour | Summary of Events and Information | Remarks and references to Appendices |
|---|---|---|---|---|
| VERMELLES | 26 Jan | 4.15 pm | Heavy hostile fire on front trenches. Battery retaliated vigorously. Quietened down at dusk. Infantry telephone wires cut. Had to run out a complete new wire. | |
| | 27* | 8 AM | Heavy hostile bombardment again on support & communication trenches. | |
| | | 2 pm | At 2 pm vigorous retaliation by all the Artillery. Fire occurred round all night on the fire roads. | |
| | 28* | 10.15 am | Hostile fire on support trenches for 10 minutes, and then a continuous fire all day on communication trenches. O.P. received a great deal of attention in the shape of about 300 rounds 4" & 2", but no damage done. The Bruyères kept up a slow rate of fire all night in the direction of the DUMP & SLAG ALLEY. | |
| | 29* | | A very foggy day. Put an end to all retaliating activity. A few odd Germans were sniped at dusk. | |
| | 30* | | Another foggy day. | |
| | 31* | | Dull & quiet day. | |

V. Stephens
O.C. "C" Battery R.F.A.

# WAR DIARY or INTELLIGENCE SUMMARY

(Erase heading not required.)

Army Form C. 2118

Vol I 1916.

Page 1

| Place | Date | Hour | Summary of Events and Information | Remarks and references to Appendices |
|---|---|---|---|---|
| VERMELLES | 1st Feb/16 | | Spasmodic artillery activity. Found gun kept up a continuous slow rate of fire all night on BILL'S BLUFF to try & keep hostile trench mortars quiet. | |
| | 2nd Feb | | Odd parties of Germans sniped at dusk & dawn, otherwise a very quiet day. We slung a mine [mortar?] at 10.45pm near HAIRPIN CRATERS. Battery carried out shoots in reply. No retaliation. We occupied crater. | |
| | 3rd Feb | | Found gun did good work among odd parties seen moving. NEW DUMP. | |
| | 4th Feb | | Particularly quiet day. Germans evidently busy improving their trenches. | |
| | 5th Feb | | Found gun sniped several parties of men moving in HAISNES – AUCHY Road – one cyclist bowled clean over. | |
| | 6th Feb | | Found guns shelled most of the morning by 15 cm of Houdringhem HAISNES and CITE ST ELIE. 200 shell with many blinds – no damage done. | |
| | 7th Feb | | Several working parties engaged. | |
| | 8th Feb | | | |
| | 9 " | | | |
| | 10 " | | | |
| | 11 " | | | |
| | 12 Feb | | Hostile artillery very quiet. Germans busy digging new front line in front of POTSDAM Trench. | |
| | 13 Feb | | We sprung a mine in the Hohenzollern. No artillery support needed. Div'l Cav Div'n commenced to be relieved by 12th Div'n. Found German shells very hard to identify; 3 bombs shattered close to them by aeroplane at dusk; enemy opens a very severe artillery fire on the KINK, KAISERIN, & buffer-northern half of ALEXANDER trench, at the German lines springing 2 mines. Hostile Infantry then tried to rush our front line trenches opposite the KINK but were driven back. At midnight German sprang another mine south of HAIRPINS. | |
| | 14th Feb | | Very high wind & gusty weather. By 15th Feb all Div'nl Cav Div'n had been relieved & except R.H.A. by 12th Division infantry. | |
| | 15th Feb | | | |
| | 16th Feb | | | |
| | 17th Feb | | | |

Army Form C. 2118

# WAR DIARY
or
INTELLIGENCE SUMMARY

Vol I 1916  Page 2

(Erase heading not required.)

| Place | Date | Hour | Summary of Events and Information | Remarks and references to Appendices |
|---|---|---|---|---|
| VERMELLES | 17 Feb | 4 AM / 1 pm | Germans strafing & more than ususal Inf in front of BIG WILLIE. At 1 pm we bombarded neighbourhood of BILLS BLUFF in conjunction with Heavy Batteries (12", 9.2", 8", 6" & 4.5"). Heavies in front line, RHA Batteries on Comm: Trenches in rear. Heavies made very good practice. Bombardment lasted for 1½ hours. Hostile retaliation very feeble, & did not commence till 9 minutes after we had opened fire. | |
| | 18th 19th 20th | | Hostile artillery very quiet. | |
| | 20th | | Found guns had then last worked at the Germans, bringing retaliation very soon after they had started firing. No 1 found gun moved to Wagon lin after dark. | |
| | 21st | | 2nd forward gun moved to Wagon line after dark. Left Section relieved by Section of 17th Battery RFA (41st Bde RFA) — Major JOLL in Command. | |
| | 22nd | 9 AM | Snow began to fall soon after 9 AM. Capt MANN rode on to SAINS LES FRESSIN, taking with him Q.M.S., & VALEDON tt Interpreter, Subsection Cooks, & Cooks Cart. | |
| | | 6.30 pm | Centre Section relieved by Section of 17th Battery. Snow stopped, but freezing hard. | |
| | | 8.30 pm | Picked up rest of Battery at SAILLI LA BOURSE. Roads very slippery. | |
| | | 12.15 AM | Passed through BETHUNE | |
| | 23rd | 3.30 AM | Halted for a few minutes at SHILAIRE. From here the roads were like glass, bitterly cold but luckily bright moon. | |
| | | 4.30 AM | Rec'd FEBVIN PALFART. Watered, unharnessed, then fed horses. Men had hot tea. | |
| | | 8 AM | Started off again. Roads getting steadily worse. Several spills but men all cheerful & doing right well. | |
| | | 10.30 AM | Passed through FRUGE | |
| SAINS LES FRESSIN | | | Arrived SAINS LES FRESSIN, without casualty to man or horse, after a long (about 40 miles) and difficult march. | |

Vol I pg 3

**WAR DIARY**
or
**INTELLIGENCE SUMMARY**
(Erase heading not required.)

Army Form C. 2118.

| Place | Date | Hour | Summary of Events and Information | Remarks and references to Appendices |
|---|---|---|---|---|
| SAINS LEZ FRESEN | February 24 | | Hard frost & snow. | |
| | 25 | | do | |
| | 26 | | Thaw set in | |
| | 27 | | General overhaul of equipment. | |
| | 28 | | | |
| | 29 | | | |

A. Parker
Capt
C "C" Battery 6-AFA

"C" Battery RHA        PAGE 1

**WAR DIARY** or **INTELLIGENCE SUMMARY**

Army Form C. 2118.

March 1916    Vol 3

| Place | Date | Hour | Summary of Events and Information | Remarks and references to Appendices |
|---|---|---|---|---|
| SAINS LEZ FRESNIN | 5th April | | During the month of March special attention was paid to the retraining of the Battery in mobile work. Cavalry Corps ceased to exist. 3rd Cavalry Division now attached to G.H.Q. | |
| | | 11th | General Campbell, Commanding 8th Cavalry Brigade, inspected the Battery in marching order. | |
| | | 13th | Lt. Colonel W. Hay D.S.O, Commanding 4th H.A. Bde came to stop with the Battery for a week. | |
| | | 14th | Leave to England opened again, 6 men per week. | |

A.L. Hutton Maj
C "C" Battery RHA.

C Bty RHA C3

Army Form C. 2118.

WAR DIARY
or
INTELLIGENCE SUMMARY. Vol 6 Page I
(Erase heading not required.)

Vol 6 Page I

| Place | Date | Hour | Summary of Events and Information | Remarks and references to Appendices |
|---|---|---|---|---|
| | June 1916 | | | |
| | 14th | | Battery took part in 6th Div. test route march & scheme | |
| | 19th | | Ditto | |
| | 24th | | Battery marched to DOMVAST and had comfortable billets arriving 1.45 AM 26th | |
| | 25th | | " " ST. LEGER " 2 AM 26th | |
| | 26th | | " " BONNAY " 4.30 AM 24th | |
| | 30th | | Battery ready to move any time after 4am, but British Offensive postponed | |

Certified true copy.

H. Cunett
MAJOR, R.H.A.
COMMANDING "C" BATTERY R.H.A.

"C" Bty RHA
Vol 4 Page 1

# WAR DIARY or INTELLIGENCE SUMMARY

Army Form C. 2118.

| Place | Date | Hour | Summary of Events and Information | Remarks and references to Appendices |
|---|---|---|---|---|
| | July 1st | | Battery kept to advance any moment at 1/5/7 am but no further orders | |
| | 7th | | Battery march to ALBERT 31 miles - billets | |
| | 8th | | Battery Southampton to CORBIE - bivouac | |
| | 9th | | Battery marching to VAUX-SUR-SOMME - bivouac | |
| | 14th | | Battery stands to at 5 am (early advance) but no breakthrough | |
| | 15th | | Same place | |
| | 19th | | Battery move to CORBIE + bivouacs at La Neuville NW of the town | |
| | ... | | [illegible] move to Arras and divide etc [illegible] | |
| | 20th 21st | | Battery trains in bivouac at La Neuville | |

M. Mann
COMMANDING "C" BATTERY, R.H.A.

C. 25 R.H.A.

Army Form C. 2118.

# WAR DIARY
## or
## INTELLIGENCE SUMMARY
*(Erase heading not required.)*

Vol 6 Page 1.

Instructions regarding War Diaries and Intelligence Summaries are contained in F. S. Regs., Part II. and the Staff Manual respectively. Title pages will be prepared in manuscript.

| Place | Date | Hour | Summary of Events and Information | Remarks and references to Appendices |
|---|---|---|---|---|
| | AUGUST | | | |
| LA NEUVILLE | 1st | 6am | March to SOUES - bivouac | |
| SOUES | 2nd | 5am | March to NEUF MOULIN - bivouac | |
| NEUF MOULIN | 4th | 4.30am | March to GRAND PREAUX - bivouac | |
| GRAND PREAUX | 5th | 6.40am | March to WAMBERCOURT - old billets occupied. | |
| WAMBERCOURT | 8th to 31st | | Battery Training with Tactical Schemes under the orders of O.C. IV Bde R.H.A. | |

Hanitt
MAJOR, R.H.A.
COMMANDING "C" BATTERY, R.H.A.

# WAR DIARY or INTELLIGENCE SUMMARY

Army Form C. 2118.

"C" R.H.A.

Summary of Events and Information during September.

| Place | Date | Hour | Summary of Events and Information | Remarks and references to Appendices |
|---|---|---|---|---|
| WIMBERCOURT | 3 Sept | | Lt H.R. Bennett is posted to 4th Bde R.H.A. H.Qrs for duty as Col. Orderly Officer. Lt Patrick R. takes over command of the Centre Section vice Boyd (E.T.) Lt Left Section | |
| " | 5 " | | Lieut Hutchins R.H. joins from Amm. Col. | |
| " | 9 " | | Right Section won competition against G & K Batteries. Won competition at Yvrencourt in Divisional Competition | |
| " | 10 " | | Battery moves to DOMINOIS into bivouack | |
| DOMINOIS | 11 " | | Battery moves to DRUCAT " " { starting 9.15 am / arriving 4.30 am | |
| DRUCAT | 12 " | | Battery moves to la CHAUSSÉE " " | |
| LA CHAUSSÉE | 13 " | | Battery remains ha CHAUSSÉE | |
| " | 14 " | | Battery moves to bivouack near BUSSY | |
| BUSSY | 15 " | | Battery moves into Z Area with 6th Cav Bde & forms to at 2 hours notice from 11 am. Z Area lies SW of BONNAY. Bivouack lught 15th 16th am to open. | |
| " | 16 " | | Same as 15th. Very little hay for the horses. | |
| " | 17 " | | Battery with 6th Cav Bde moves to a new bivouack South of | |

Army Form C. 2118.

# WAR DIARY
## or
## INTELLIGENCE SUMMARY.
*(Erase heading not required.)*

Vol 9  Page 2

Instructions regarding War Diaries and Intelligence Summaries are contained in F.S. Regs., Part II. and the Staff Manual respectively. Title pages will be prepared in manuscript.

| Place | Date | Hour | Summary of Events and Information | Remarks and references to Appendices |
|---|---|---|---|---|
| QUERRIEU | 17th Sept | | QUERRIEU. | |
| " | 18 & 19 | | Very Wet - Horse lines Swamp - obtained 13 tents | |
| " | 20 | | Weather clearing though still raining | |
| " | 22 | | Battery moves to SOUES. | |
| SOUES | 23rd | | Battery moves to BEAUCOURT near AUXI-LE-CHATEAU & Bivouacks in good ground. | |
| BEAUCOURT | 24 | | Battery marches via AUXI-LE-CHATEAU & the North bank of the RIVER AUTHIE to DOURIEZ | |
| DOURIEZ | 25 & 26 | | | |
| | 29 | | Battery marches to AIRON ST VAAST. | |
| | 30 | | AIRON ST VAAST | |
| | | | Extract from Part II Orders No 14 d/ 9 Sept. 1916. | |
| | | | No 68817 - By: Jeffery E. Awarded Military Medal for Distinguished service in the field. handed on Gazette d/ 3. 6. 16. | |

H Catlett

COMMANDING ?O? BATTERY, R.H.?

Army Form C. 2118.

# WAR DIARY
## or
## INTELLIGENCE SUMMARY.
(Erase heading not required.)

Nov 1916  "C" Battery, 2 RHA

Vol 10

| Place | Date | Hour | Summary of Events and Information | Remarks and references to Appendices |
|---|---|---|---|---|
| MESNIL | | 1st | Attack on BEAUMONT-HAMEL & BEAUCOURT postponed till 5th Nov. | |
| | | 5th | Attack unsuccessful. Postponed owing to bad weather conditions | |
| | | 13th | Attack takes place. (Battery to act as action after successfully barraging in enfilade for Hughes immediately S. of St PIERRE DIVION at 3Bry + 1 hour. The IV Bde RHA concentrates in AVELUY WOOD Major Scarlett & Lt Chapman Reconnoitred advanced difficulties in the way of machine guns + shell fire & position near HAMEL. About 2pm the battery was ordered back to THIEPVAL about 2pm in order to barrage Kneefup N. of BEAUCOURT as a Counter attack was expected. The battery came into action at about 3pm near the old position carried out its new task. | |
| | | 15th | Battery advances & came into action near HAMEL - wagon line still remains between ENGREBEMER & HEDAUVILLE. | |
| | | 17th | Wagon line advances to S. of St pt AVELUY WOOD | |
| | | 20th | bivr. Messines suddenly that the battery had to evacuate its position at 5.30 p.m. it took with them all ammunition at the gun line & got away from gun position from 1am to 5.30 am 21st another enemy. | |

Army Form C. 2118.

"C" Battery R.H.A.

# WAR DIARY
## or
## INTELLIGENCE SUMMARY.
*(Erase heading not required.)*

| Place | Date | Hour | Summary of Events and Information | Remarks and references to Appendices |
|---|---|---|---|---|
| AVELUY | 21st | | Bau leaves on lorries. Battery marches to MARIEUX arriving at about 1.30 p.m. Owing to the hard frost has roads & billets for the night, the horses were quartered in family huts & tiles, one of the huts that they had ever been in. "K" & "G" were billeted in the same village | |
| MARIEUX | | | | |
| BERTAUCOURT | 22nd | | Battery marches to BERTAUCOURT & billets for night. "C" "G" "K" "H" & "I" were all billeted in this village | |
| ST RIQUIER | 23rd | | Battery marches to ST RIQUIER occupying the same area as when here in May. All IV "Bde & "A" & "I" Bre Batteries there. 5 RHA Batteries have their are the only occasions on which 5 RHA batteries have billeted in the same village. | |
| ROUSSENT | 24th -30th | | Battery marches to ROUSSENT & go into permanent billets. General business of cleaning up all round. | |

COMMANDING "C" BATTERY R.H.A.

# WAR DIARY or INTELLIGENCE SUMMARY

Army Form C. 2118.

C Bty RHA Vol XI

## DECEMBER 1916

| Place | Date | Hour | Summary of Events and Information | Remarks and references to Appendices |
|---|---|---|---|---|
| ROUSSEL | 15 | 6.15ᵃᵐ | Time spent in building stables & grooming | |
| R... | 16 | | Battery marched to Renty & billetted through the night | |
| AIRE | 17 | | Battery marched to AIRE and billetted 16"-17" Prince Ruper Cavalry Barracks on the SW outskirts of the town. We found strangely little (as) + no Section's horses were in the op-... |  |
| AIRE | 18-31 | | Battery led an idyllic existence. Attended the 1st Army ARTILLERY School which was a fortnight of the funniest kind of lectures [illeg]. Men had comfortable quarters and officers living at an hotel kept tight. Van M[?] 15 th Regt were the Staff and a number of big-wigs, [illeg] and also attended. XI & C ... Lucy, Oldham, Eastman, Arthur-Jones ... Baillie trip [illeg]... Scotch & Irish cork-flows Dump dump... Stud Book Punch & etc were in Very Satisfactory [illeg] | |

H. Corbett
MAJOR, R.H.A.
COMMANDING "C" BATTERY R.H.A.

# WAR DIARY
## or
## INTELLIGENCE SUMMARY.
(Erase heading not required.)

Army Form C. 2118.

Jan. 1917 "C" Battery, R.H.A.
Vol XII

| Place | Date | Hour | Summary of Events and Information | Remarks and references to Appendices |
|---|---|---|---|---|
| AIRE | 1st | | "C" Battery remained at 1st ARMY ARTILLERY School. Horses & vehicles were used almost daily for School Purposes. | |
| | 31st | | | |

W. Thwain
Capt R.H.A.

# WAR DIARY or INTELLIGENCE SUMMARY

Army Form C. 2118.

C Bar RHA Vol 13

| Place | Date | Hour | Summary of Events and Information | Remarks and references to Appendices |
|---|---|---|---|---|
| AIRE | 1.28 | | C Battery was situated at Dafsil Valley about 13th Mikiny ARTILLERY SCHOOL | |
| | 26 Jan 1917 | | Lt. N.E. Chapman left the Battery & proceeded to | |
| | 27" Feb | | 2nd Army at Cassel for G. Battery RHA | |
| | 3" | | Lt. J.T. Boylan left the Valley Ashia to IV Bde RHA | |
| | | | Lt. H.G. Munson has joined "C" Battery Vice Chapman | |
| | | | wounded was attached to HORSE ARTILLERY 3.2.17 | |
| | 6" | | J.R. Patterson RFA posted from HQ 28" Bde RFA | |
| | 9" | | at Stroyars 107 Jd26 to "G" to "C" Vice Boylan | |
| | | | from D/SI Brig RFA "C" Battery joining from Sick Court | |
| | | | Stoppages of punishments (regulation) 3 2.1.17 | |
| | | | No 54796 Gnr hogg F. 1 Awarded Military Medal for | |
| | | | No 125.04 Cr Mackay W. J Bravery in the field | |
| | | | Lt H Munson Capt RHA |

Army Form C. 2118.

# WAR DIARY
## or
## INTELLIGENCE SUMMARY.
(Erase heading not required.)

MARCH 1917

| Place | Date | Hour | Summary of Events and Information | Remarks and references to Appendices |
|---|---|---|---|---|
| AIRE | 1st | | 1st Army Artillery School | |
| | 2nd | | do | |
| | 3rd | | do | |
| | 4th | | do | |
| DENNE BROEUCQ | 5th | | Left AIRE 9am. Heavy snow. Arrived DENNEBROEUCQ 12.30pm | |
| | 6th | | Left DENNEBROEUCQ 9am arrived LESPINOY 1pm. rejoined 6th Cav. Bde. | |
| | 7th | | LESPINOY | |
| | 8th | | | |
| | 9th till | | | |
| | 22nd | | Bdr: Route march for Gen Vaughan 3rd Cav. Div. | |
| | 23rd | | marched to MERIMONT 13 miles, for Practice. | |
| | 24th | | Fired 3 series. Shrapnel. & H.E. | |
| | 25th | | 2 " " " & H.E. 141 Shrapnel 50 H.E. | |
| | 26th till | | returned to LESPINOY. | |
| | 31st | | LESPINOY. Weather bad all month. | |

H Scott W? M?? Lt RHA
COMMANDING "C" BATTERY R.H.A.

**Army Form C. 2118.**

"C" Bty R.H.a.

# WAR DIARY
or
INTELLIGENCE SUMMARY.
*(Erase heading not required.)*

APRIL 1917                    Vol 15

Instructions regarding War Diaries and Intelligence Summaries are contained in F.S. Regs., Part II. and the Staff Manual respectively. Title pages will be prepared in manuscript.

| Place | Date | Hour | Summary of Events and Information | Remarks and references to Appendices |
|---|---|---|---|---|
| LESPINOY | 1st | | Sgt Ladd and Gunner MAHADY paraded with Mixed Bridal at tennis of G.O.C. 3rd Cav Bde. at MARESQUEZ 12 noon. (for work in 1915) | |
| " | 2nd - 4th | | Men and horses under cover. | |
| CONTES | 5th | 10 am | Left LESPINOY 10am arrived CONTES 12 noon. 5 miles. | |
| CONTES | 6th | | Orders to move cancelled. | |
| VERQUERIE | 7th | 9 am | Left CONTES 9am. arrived VERQUERIE 2.30pm. Men & horses under cover. 15 miles. | |
| LE BOURG FOSSEUX | 8th | 2 pm | Left VERQUERIE at 2pm arrived FOSSEUX at 7pm 17 miles. Men in huts - horses in open. Watering places very poor. Water cart broke in two on march. G.B. wagon pole broke. | |
| ARRAS | 9th | 7.30 am | Stood to at 7.30am. Moved at 10 am through Western edge of ARRAS where we halted at 4.30pm. O.C. accompanied G.O.C. 6th Bde. to a point H.35.d.40. ref. 1/40,000 51B. Bivouacked in ARRAS at 8pm. Sent horses to water, but did not return till 10.30pm. Receiving orders arrived at 11.15pm to move out of ARRAS at 11.30pm. Moved to a pit on ST.POL- ARRAS road 6 miles out of ARRAS. No shelter for men or horses. | |

# WAR DIARY
## or
## INTELLIGENCE SUMMARY.
(Erase heading not required.)

Army Form C. 2118.

| Place | Date | Hour | Summary of Events and Information | Remarks and references to Appendices |
|---|---|---|---|---|
| | 10th | | Moved out of camp at 11am. Went at a foot pace through ARRAS and along the CAVALRY Track towards FEUCHY CHAPEL. Adv. Battery along ARRAS-CAMBRAI Rd. Brought Battery into action at H.34.c.11 at 4p.m. Wagon lines 500 yds back along the ARRAS-CAMBRAI Rd. and N.9.b.it. Snowing heavily. No shelter. | |
| | 11th | | Ready to move forward at 5.30am. at 6am. 8th Cav. Bde. moved forward to their objective N. of MONCHY le PREAUX and 6th 13 de followed. 2nd D.Gs leading with objective S. of MONCHY le PREAUX. Lt Patrick and left section accompanied 3rd D.Gs remainder of Battery followed Royals on to ORANGE HILL. Rt section joined left section and left sections came into action to support 3rd DGs at N.6.c.5.1. Retired on to ORANGE HILL at 2 pm. Wagon lines on ORANGE HILL shelled and retired below ridge. Battery of 3rd Cav. Div. were now divisionalized & took up positions on ORANGE HILL. Our position was N.9.d.5.5. Showers had orders for R.H.A. to retire to ARRAS Race COURSE at 7pm. | |

# WAR DIARY or INTELLIGENCE SUMMARY.

(Erase heading not required.)

Army Form C. 2118.

| Place | Date | Hour | Summary of Events and Information | Remarks and references to Appendices |
|---|---|---|---|---|
| | 11/72 | | Owing to congestion on ARRAS road, progress slow. Total casualties during day. N.C.O.s & men 18. Horses 27. Staff Sgt. Janier Watson & S.S. Fitter Palmer both (seriously) wounded. (Includes 3 men killed). | |
| FOSSEAUX | 12/72 | | Arrived at rate course at 3 a.m. but finding no one turned back on to St Pol Road. Blizzard from 4 a.m. till 5 a.m. Very cold. Officers N.C.O.s & men also horses another done up. Took out horses at 5.30 a.m. and fed. No clothes, and left of mud. At 9.30 a.m. moved on to FOSSEAUX 13 miles. Arrived 2 p.m. Very cold wind. | |
| FOSSEAUX | 13/72 | | | |
| " | 14/72 | | Men had difficulty in getting on their boots again. Horses in deep mud. | |
| " | 15/72 | | | |
| BOUFFLERS | 16/72 | | Marched out at 5 a.m. reached BOUFFLERS at 5 p.m. (28 miles) | |
| " | 17/72 | | | |
| " | 18 | | | |

Army Form C. 2118.

Instructions regarding War Diaries and Intelligence Summaries are contained in F. S. Regs., Part II. and the Staff Manual respectively. Title pages will be prepared in manuscript.

# WAR DIARY
or
## INTELLIGENCE SUMMARY.
(Erase heading not required.)

| Place | Date | Hour | Summary of Events and Information | Remarks and references to Appendices |
|---|---|---|---|---|
| ROUSSENT | 19th | | Left BOUFFLERS at 8.15am arrived ROUSSENT at 1.30pm (15 miles) | |
| " | 20th | | | |
| till | 30th | | | |

H Marwitham[?]
30/4/17.

SUPPLIMENTARY WAR DIARY.
MAP Reference Sheet 51B 1/40,000.

Orders to be ready to move at 5.30 a.m.
As Battn. Hdqrs. moved up along ARRAS - CAMBRAI road a shell fell near No 3
Teams killing 2 men and wounding 6. 7 horses also killed and wounded.
The X roads W of FEUCHY CHAPEL and the ground W of FEUCHY CHAPEL hill
was under shell fire from some 5.9 batteries at odd moments during
the day. The S.S. Davies and S.S. Fetter were seriously wounded r
at 9.30 a.m. the 8th Bde. moved forward followed by the 6th Bde. 3rd D.G.S
leading, accompanied by Left Section and Lt Patrick.
At 11 a.m. the Rt. Section joined the Left Section and the Battery was brought
into action to cover the 3rd D.G.S. at N8c51. The 3rd D.G.S. held the high
ground from MONCHY & FOSSE FARM, joining up with 8th Bde at MONCHY.
Our line ran roughly as follows:- O14b0. - LABERGERE - N12d - 18a - 17d - 17a.6.6
but the situation esp. on the Rt flank was not very clear.
The sloping ground between ORANGE HILL and FOSSE FARM was exposed to machine
gun fire and shrapnel fire from the direction of GUEMAPPE.
The position taken up by the 4 guns was a covered one, about 6 ft of cover in front
and hidden by FOSSE FARM on the right. Flashes would have been visible from

2.

The high ground behind HENINEL and GUEMAPPE.
The wagon lines were placed on the low ground between Hq Battery and FOSSE FARM.
Heads of horses facing the Battery. The 3rd B.C. horses were also here.
The Sgt. Major was sent to steady the horses as FOSSE FARM came under heavy shell fire from BOIS du SART and BOIS du VERT. (4.2 shell)
Lt Patrick directed the fire of the Battery from a pit in N.12.b. by telephone.
Targets engaged. Infantry in wood at 08h.h. also machine gun.
German Infantry digging in front of Bois du SART & Bois du VERT.
Ranging about 60. In consultation with A.C. 3rd B.C.s it was decided to save ammunition in case of German attack.

About 12.30 p.m. 5 German planes flew over position. One flying very low.
These planes remained in manoeuvre about 15 minutes.
The Staff Capt. (?) Cav'y Bde was with me. You got near the Battery as did the 3rd A.D.C. and took back a statement to the G.O.C. Cavalry Bde
a/c. 1 Coy 4 Bn of Infantry came down the Slopes from ORANGE HILL
towards the position. They were shelled by H.E. & Shrapnel and retired. Few casualties. Several thousands MONCHY.
About 1.30 p.m. orders were received for the Battery to withdraw to ORANGE HILL
from 8ce B.C.S. Bde. The withdrawal was carried out under shell fire.
The Battery again came under machine [gun] & shrapnel fire passing the
windmill on ORANGE HILL.
The wagons and centre section left on ORANGE HILL were also
shelled by Hospital aeroplanes and were heavily shelled.

3

These Majors and Bom returned under Lt. HUTCHINS in good order, and took up a position held the FEUCHY Ridge.

Batteries were now disineantegged and the R+L left sections took up a position about NU455, about 3 p.m.

A Telephone wire was run out to the Eastern slope of ORANGE Hill, but about 300 yards were invisible E of MONCHY, except from St. Patrick's & first O.P. Fire was directed on to Bois du VERT and road E of LA BERGERE where German Cavalry were spotted. Rounds fired roughly 400. Snow fell heavily.

The B.S.M. was now sent to the Wagon lines to take the horses to water and Lt Hutching was sent to refill ammunition from ARRAS. He also thought that the field dressings on many of ours had been mixed up. He being at night. Some unable shell fire and one driver was killed and one wounded. The Major later again came under shell fire from 5.30 p.m. till 6.30 p.m., but the B.S.M. decided not to move them, as all informed had and FEUCHY Ridge was without a shell fire any how. Orders were received to move back to ARRAS RACECOURSE.

Total casualties. O.R. killed 3. wounded 16.
Horses killed and wounded 27.

Army Form C. 2118.

"L" Battery ?H?A

Vol 16

# WAR DIARY
or
## INTELLIGENCE SUMMARY
(Erase heading not required.)

May 1917

| Place | Date | Hour | Summary of Events and Information | Remarks and references to Appendices |
|---|---|---|---|---|
| ROUSSENT | 1st-12th | | Grazing | |
| | 6th | | "L" Cav Bde Horse Show. No 200 Won Brigade Jumping Competition open to Brigade Farriers + W.O's. Ridden by 2Lt CHANDLER | |
| | 10th | | Battery received following numbers of Remounts from the Cavalry to replace Casualties.  N.S.Y. - 5   H.Q. 6th Cav Bde - 1   3rd D. Gds - 9   1st Royals - 8   Essex Yeo. - 2 | |
| TORTE FONTAINE | | | Battery marches to TORTE FONTAINE & bivouaches for night | |
| OUTRE BOIS | 13th | | " " " OUTRE BOIS | |
| HAVERNAS | 14th | | " " " HAVERNAS | |
| BUSSY LES DAOURS | 15th | | " " " BUSSY LES DAOURS | |
| HARBONNIERS | 16th | | " " " HARBONNIERS | |
| ROISEL | 17th | | " " " ROISEL & bivouaches | |
| Aug?? of | 21st 22nd | | | |
| " | " 23rd | | Nos 4 & 5 Subsections went into action at RONSOY | |
| | | | ? ? ? into action at RONSOY | |

Army Form C. 2118.

E Battery RHA

# WAR DIARY
## or
## INTELLIGENCE SUMMARY.
(Erase heading not required.)

| Place | Date | Hour | Summary of Events and Information | Remarks and references to Appendices |
|---|---|---|---|---|
| | 29th | 10pm | WAGON LINE remained at Roisel. The position of the guns in action was in old German gun-in-action pits. These camouflaged nets with turf between. Very little digging was done as with wish to attract in any way the surrounding C.B. did not wish it to be known that 30 guns in this position. Shelters had been made about the position. When the position was first discovered by the enemy though it was much turning fast discovered by the enemy though it was much turning hollow advance launcher position. All above positions Lt Thomson - section above position New of Ransor House. Balloon observation to get to within close range. | |
| | 30th | 3" | All guns in action in above positions. | |
| | 23rd 31st | 9" | The guns were layed at night on a barrage line which after 26th October ran from X 30 a 1.7 to X 30 c 5.9 to X 6 a 4 0. | |

E.M.Rann
Capt RHA

# WAR DIARY
## INTELLIGENCE SUMMARY

"C" Battery R.H.A.

June 1917

VI / 1 / 7

**Army Form C. 2118.**

6. Last night 19-20th Essex Yeomanry raided enemy SAP about X30.a.6.6. The battery cooperated successfully with a barrage on the S.O.S. line

6. Night 24-25th The Royals raided the enemy trenches between O5950 & CANAL WOODS. The battery took part firing up a barrage in & about 0555 WOOD

6. A great deal of work was done by the battery in the position & Sgt Goldsmith with the cooperation of Sgt Wellbelove made a camouflaged position for 4 guns about FI8.C.8.4. to the left front of the position occupied by the battery

E. Ingham
Capt RHA

Army Form C. 2118.

# WAR DIARY
## or
## INTELLIGENCE SUMMARY

(Erase heading not required.)

| Place | Date | Hour | Summary of Events and Information | Remarks and references to Appendices |
|---|---|---|---|---|
| RONSOY | 4th | 10 pm | Battery remains in action in position S.E. of Ronsoy & section in ENFER WOOD | |
| | 4th | 11 pm | Position at Ronsoy had two units. Right section in ENFER WOOD wounds been fixed after shell delay owing to Gas Alarm | |
| RONSSOY | 5th | 12.30 pm | Whole Battery had assembled at Wagon lines near Ronsoy where it remained for the night. | |
| BUIRE | 5th | | Battery marches to Buire when it camped in the 6th Cav. Bde Area next door to the 6th Machine Gun Squadron | |
| | 7th | | Brigade Tactical Exercise. Signallers only took part | |
| | 8th | | Battery bay places under the asst Dr. C. RHA 2nd Cav Div | |
| | 8th | 10.30 pm | No left section turns W.P. patch went into action on 8th horse lop C/o 4 Ronsoy occupying to right two spits. D, E & J Batteries & the 3rd Bde RHA Column supplied the section with ammunition | |
| | | | The transport of the Battery (Xxxxx) at BUIRE H.W. Baker RHA the latest of 28.5.17 has taken a fatigue party to KNFER WOOD to have a trench dug out as far as 7 & 8 Cav. M.G. batteries | |
| | 9 | 12 noon | W section registered on A.7b, a dead horse TREE hut giving view to Battery Hq & damaged column between KNOLL & GUILLEMONT FARM. | |

Army Form C. 2118.

R Battery R.H.A.

# WAR DIARY
## or
## INTELLIGENCE SUMMARY.
(Erase heading not required.)

| Place | Date | Hour | Summary of Events and Information | Remarks and references to Appendices |
|---|---|---|---|---|
| RUISSOY / BUIRE | 10 | 4.15am | Raid by GREYS on GUILLEMONT FARM. F.8 & English Section W.Arty fired abt 300 rounds. H Section 7 rounds to festive & returned to BUIRE when alerted. | |
| | | 3am | Gunners arrived at 6 gun H. Hotchkiss took the Right Section in F.8 was FRENY relieving a section of "K" Battery. | |
| | | 7pm | W Bties took over Command of the Section of "K" Battery in action in F.8 relieving a | |
| BUIRE / FRENY | 11 | | Centre Section Major St Kearn's came in action in F.8 relieving a Section of K Battery | |
| BUIRE / ERMEN | | 10pm | 11 P. Baker took his Wag a line from BUIRE to a position you Route close to the Post. Un summary it was in Intervention of 5th June | |
| RUISSOY / FRENY | 12 | 11/m | Relieving Section (the left) plus of "K" Battery 3rd Section F.8 & Capt H.M.Bryan has been in Command of the Composite battery based on Command to Capt S.H.Brown. | |
| | 12½ | | The Battery returned in action in F.B. with the Wagon Line near the Houses The Battery Bomb had the German trenches - Ghost | |
| | 3" | | the BIRDCAGE about X30 a b.c. Several raids took place. | |

Army Form C. 2118.

R. Battery RHA

Vol 1/8

# WAR DIARY
## or
## INTELLIGENCE SUMMARY.
(Erase heading not required.)

| Place | Date | Hour | Summary of Events and Information | Remarks and references to Appendices |
|---|---|---|---|---|
| | JULY 1917 | | | |
| YPCHY | 1st-7th | | Battery remained in action supporting the 2nd Coy in the letting A Raid took place on GUILLEMONT in which the letting captured successfully. | |
| KOISEL | 7-10 | | Battery remained wagon lines. | |
| BRAY | 11th | | Battery marched to BRAY via PERONNE-BIACHES-HERBÉCOURT. Distance 20 Miles Time 6 hours. Water & fees PERONNE Order of March "E" "C" "K" "G" | |
| SARTON | 12 | | Battery (Major L.) & SARTON & was halted 1½ hour at MARIEUX to help the road clear for the King. Route - ALBERT - BOUZINCOURT - BAZENTIN 19½ Miles Time 7½ hrs Order of March G. C. K. Water & Fees MARKET | |
| LUCHEUX WARLING | 13 | | Battery bivouacked at L'Etre Warlin - Route ORVILLE - LUCHEUX ect Distance 12 miles Time 4 hours. Order of March G. K. C | |
| HEPPICOURT | 14 | | Battery to HERNICOURT via Monchiétry - St Pol - Order of March "C" "G". Distance 11 miles. Time 3 hours. Heavy Thunderstorm - Collapse of sheds. | |

Army Form C. 2118.

A Battery RHA

# WAR DIARY
or
## INTELLIGENCE SUMMARY.
(Erase heading not required.)

| Place | Date | Hour | Summary of Events and Information | Remarks and references to Appendices |
|---|---|---|---|---|
| | August 15th | | Battery marches to Auchel. Miles - Max Time 5 hours | |
| La Motte Baudet | 16 | | Battery marches to La Motte Baudet 1½ miles NE of St Venant. Distance 12½ m. Time 5 hours. | |
| 16 6.3.9 | | | Battery (arrived) at La Motte Baudet. On the 2nd Brigade Horse Show took place. Battery won the following Events Walk Polo 1st 220 yards 1st Officers too yards 1st & 2nd 220 yards Open 1st | |

C.J.H. avery
Capt. RHA.

Army Form C. 2118.

# WAR DIARY
or
## INTELLIGENCE SUMMARY.
(Erase heading not required.)

"L" Battery R.H.A.

VII 19

| Place | Date | Hour | Summary of Events and Information | Remarks and references to Appendices |
|---|---|---|---|---|
| CAMP #13 BRUAY - 80 | August 1917 | | This period was marked by various training exercises. 1) Crossing Canal Mon Tête Naz acqueduct de la Mischte 500 yards E. of the place in which similar exercises took place in 1915. Cav. Corps Commander was present. 2) Route marching in Box-Respirators (3) C.O.s three over 18 months without leave went on 10 days leave during a period of 28 days. Check of Equipment. Check of the number of rifles on the battery establishment took place from 36 to 98. 25. Divisional Horse Show. Battery was 3rd in the Gun Team Competition. Battery was 3rd in the Roms hyr Comp. Battery exercises regarding STOMEK + attack on Rifle Rouge (certain new tactics in the Infantry attacks. | |

W.H. ...... Capt R.H.A.

O. Battery R.H.A.
September 1917
Vol 20

# WAR DIARY
or
# INTELLIGENCE SUMMARY

(Erase heading not required.)

Army Form C. 2118.

| Place | Date | Hour | Summary of Events and Information | Remarks and references to Appendices |
|---|---|---|---|---|
| ST OMER | 1st | | SEPTEMBER 1917 Battery marches to NIEURLET near ST MOMELIN & billets there | |
| ST MOMELIN | 2nd | | Guns & instructors here lent to the 5th ARMY RESERVE DIVISIONAL ARTILLERY V Corps for training purposes | |
| HERZEELE | 6th | | Battery moves to the HERZEELE AREA & billets in Mynhackes about 2 miles N.W. of the town | |
| | 14th | | Battery marches to Belgium billets N.E. of HERZEELE near Hondschoote on River YSER | |
| | 17th | | Guns lent out to 77th & 84th Bdes R.F.A. | |
| 17th–30th | | | Gun available for firing reconnaissance schemes &c. Lbs Respirators were worn & a good deal of gundrill & a fair amount of jumping with jumps were put up & took place. | |

C.M.Grant
Capt. R.H.A.

# WAR DIARY
## ~~INTELLIGENCE SUMMARY~~

"C" Battery R.H.A.
October 1917

Army Form C. 2118.

| Place | Date | Hour | Summary of Events and Information | Remarks and references to Appendices |
|---|---|---|---|---|
| WIRZEELE | 1st | | Guns & horses thrown out to 282nd R.F.A (Territorial) Brigade. A very excellent football match was played against A/282 but results were two to us 2 - nil. The Colonel & officers of "A" the called & went round our jumps. | A/282 |
| | 2nd | | Capt. J. Chisnum de Xasteus lu hadu on leave. Lt. Col. J Get an interview with Genl (Anderson) | |
| | 5th | | Received orders the move to ST MOMELIN AREA | |
| | 6th | | Battery marched to ST MOMELIN & billetes in Rouge-Creusson Farm adjoining farms. | |
| | 6th – 31st | | This Period was spent in cleaning guns & instructors to Army Field Artillery Brigades. | |

W.A.[illegible]
Capt. R.H.A.

6/3 Cav.

"C" Battery RHA

# WAR DIARY
## or
## INTELLIGENCE SUMMARY.
(Erase heading not required.) "C" Battery RHA.

Army Form C. 2118.

| Place | Date | Hour | Summary of Events and Information | Remarks and references to Appendices |
|---|---|---|---|---|
| DAILY MAIL WOOD near BAYONCOURT | August 1918. | | | |
| | 1st | | Battery bivouaced with remainders of H.M. Bde RHA in reserve to III Corps | |
| | 5th 6th 7th | | Marched from Daily mail wood to PETIT ST JEAN west of AMIENS to rejoin 6th Cav Bde who marched in by night. Marched with 6th Cav Bde at 9.30 p.m. to concentration area east of LONGUEAU in connection with operations being carried out on IVth Army | |
| | 8th | 4.20 AM | moved forward about 5.0 AM. 6th Cav Bde was in reserve to 3rd Cav Divn who was leading Divisions. Two hours Advance slowly over track via CACHY- RIFLE WOOD- DEMUIN past a position near CAIX where Battery had been in action in March 1918. Baignet no shelling anywhere near Battery went into action about 5.0 PM about 1 mile S of CAIX to support 6th Cav Bde holding line East of Le QUESNEL fired one stonk & SOS also registration and enemy | |
| | 9th | | Battery accompanied 6th Cav Bde to reserve on Rural LACE between CAVEUX and IGANAOCOURT where reserved by infantry At two shell fell into wagon lines on morning of 9th. I man slightly wounded to horse hit | |
| | 10th | 5.30 AM | Remained in reserve till 5.30AM on 10th E.A. very active with bombs and H.V. guns moved 5.30 AM with 6th Cav Bde towards LE QUESNEL thence to FOLIES. Lt. Sechern under Lieut Bonker attached with 3rd Dragoons Guards moved to LE QUESNOY. But did not get an opportunity of getting into action. Remainder of Battery remained near FOLIES. | |
| | 11th | 7.0 PM | Left behor reserved about 7.0 PM 6th Cav Bde bivouaced might areas FOLIES. E.A. very active bombing Remained in reserve at FOLIES till 5.15 PM Advance held up at PARVILLES country east of FOLIES impossible for mounted troops, drung edge of old SOMME battlefield 6th Cav Bde moved to FOUENCAMPS S.E. of AMIENS arriving 3.0 AM 12th. | |
| | 12th 13th 14th 15th 16th | | French in FOUENCAMPS. C in C. F.M. Sir Douglas Haig visited Bde and came round Battery. Remained FOUENCAMPS. Battery moved with Bde to LE MESGE East of AMIENS marching at 9.0 pm arriving LE MESGE about 10 AM. | |

Army Form C. 2118.

# WAR DIARY
## or
## INTELLIGENCE SUMMARY.
(Erase heading not required.)

Instructions regarding War Diaries and Intelligence Summaries are contained in F.S. Regs., Part II. and the Staff Manual respectively. Title pages will be prepared in manuscript.

| Place | Date | Hour | Summary of Events and Information | Remarks and references to Appendices |
|---|---|---|---|---|
| | 17th 18th 19th 20th | | Remained LENEGGE good camp horses doing well. | |
| | 21st | | Marched with 6th Cav Bde. 12 midnight to FIEFFES S.W. of DOULLENS. No billets | |
| | 22nd | 2.0 AM | Arrived FIEFFES | |
| | 23rd 24th 25th 26th | | Remained FIEFFES Moved with 6th Cav Bde to WILLENCOURT NW of AUXI-LE-CHATEAU. Marching 8 P.M. | |
| | 26th | 3.6 AM | Arrived WILLENCOURT | |
| | 27th | | Moved to PETIT BOURET east of FREVENT. On 1 hour to move in connection with operations east of ARRAS changed to 3 hours notice. Later in day | |
| | 28th | | on 3 hours notice | |
| | 29th | | Orders to move to WAILLY S W of ARRAS orders cancelled | |
| | 30th | | on short notice to move to WAILLY. Part on 6 hours notice and ordered to commence training scheme for use of Cavalry in ARRAS operation being suspended | |
| | 31st | | Remained PETIT BOURET. No changes in Battery during month. Arrival of the new armament with P.M.O. required. Horses kept in good condition in spite of long night marches. Lieut. Longland evacuated towards end of month | |

A.5634 Wt. W.4973/M687 750,000 8/16 D. D. & L. Ltd. Forms/C.2118/13.

Army Form C. 2118.

# WAR DIARY
## or
## INTELLIGENCE SUMMARY.
(Erase heading not required.)

"C" Battery R.H.A.   SEPTEMBER 1918

Instructions regarding War Diaries and Intelligence Summaries are contained in F.S. Regs. Part II. and the Staff Manual respectively. Title pages will be prepared in manuscript.

| Place | Date | Hour | Summary of Events and Information | Remarks and references to Appendices |
|---|---|---|---|---|
| R. BOURET | 1st | | Battery with 6th Cav: Bde. on 6 hours notice to move | |
| | 2nd | | on 1 hour notice to move. In connection with c/ammo dump ARRAS | |
| | 3rd | | Notice changed to 2 hours. Later changed to 6 hour | |
| | 4th | | Positions & training of young Gunners | |
| | 5th | | | |
| | 6th | | Battery moved with 6th Cav: Bde. Bombay Rd billet at FRESNOY nr HESDIN | |
| | 7th | | Training continued. Gas on instr'n permitted | |
| | 14th | | | |
| | 15th | | | |
| | 16th | | Bombay moved to Pierronne at Pt ST LEU | |
| | 17th | | Took part in Cav Corps manoeuvres. Enclud day at Noir AUXI-LE-CHATEAU | |
| | | | Marched to Bouverez at LE QUESNEL. Firm War OUTREMIS. Horses covered in the distance approx 35 miles | |
| FRESNOY | | | March to FRESNOY both following | |
| | 18th | | Moved to BONNIÈRES in FREVENT area | |
| | 19th | | Contd. March to FORTEL Coy. Buchan and CA in La R. FORTEL | |
| | 30th | | all horse linens ever | |

A5834. Wt W4973/M687 750,000 8/16 D.D.&L.Ltd. Forms/C.2118/13.

Army Form C. 2118.

# WAR DIARY
## or
## INTELLIGENCE SUMMARY.

(Erase heading not required.) SEPTEMBER 1918.

C Battery R.H.A.

| Place | Date | Hour | Summary of Events and Information | Remarks and references to Appendices |
|---|---|---|---|---|
| FORTEL | 21st 22 23 24 | | Remained at FORTEL and ROEFLATS | |
| | 25" 26" | | Pontoon bridge with 6th C.B. Billeted at ST LEGER LES AUTHIE. Arrived at above place at 04.40 a.m. | |
| | 26" | | Marched to Rainville at MEAULTE. Arriving O.O. 15t 28" | |
| | 27" | | Marched to HEM. Arriving 28.50 | |
| | 28" | | Remained HEM | |
| | 29" | | Moved at 14.30 to VETMAND in terrace to supply operations about BELLENGLISE & BELLICOURT. | |
| | 30" | | Remained VETMAND | |
| | | | Lieut HUTCHINS RFA and Lt O.L Booer M.C. RFA Returned fr leave from England on 13" inst | |

JS Law
Capt R.H.A
for O.C. C Battery R.H.A.

**WAR DIARY** or **INTELLIGENCE SUMMARY**
(Erase heading not required.)

**CONFIDENTIAL**, Army Form C. 2118.

C Bty RHA

OCTOBER 1918

| Place | Date | Hour | Summary of Events and Information | Remarks and references to Appendices |
|---|---|---|---|---|
| | 1st | | Battery concen. for the with 6th Cav Bde about VERMAND | Ref 1/100,000 ST QUENTIN Sheet 18 VALENCIENNES Sheet 12 |
| | 2nd | | Marched 08.30 hr to BELLENGLISE, returned to VERMAND about 12.50. No scheme took place actual. | |
| | 3rd | | Stood to at 8.30 hrs. moved to valley near MAGNY LA FOSSE at 15.00 Regtl Section went on with 3 Dragoon Guards and came into action 500 yds N. of P of PRESSELLES and engaged enemy counter attack at 1600 yards. Casualties 1 man Lt in chest. Battery retired to Bivouac at ST HELENE for the night. | |
| | 4th | | Stood to at 6am. But did not move. | |
| | 5th 6th 7th | | Battery moved to billets at TREFCON with "A" Bde. Remained TREFCON. | |
| | 8th | | Marched at 04.30 from TREFCON to valley near MAGNY-LA-FOSSE, and on to NE of ESTREES about 13.00 hrs. returned to valley near MAGNY LA FOSSE for night. | 8/10/1918 |
| | 9th | | Marched off 05.00 hrs to BEAUREVOIR after however half moved on via PREMONT to MARETZ. Reo joining S/B Bde. | 9/10/1918 |

# WAR DIARY
## or
## INTELLIGENCE SUMMARY

Army Form C. 2118.

E Battery R.H.A.

OCTOBER 1918

| Place | Date | Hour | Summary of Events and Information | Remarks and references to Appendices |
|---|---|---|---|---|
| | 9th | | Came into action against enemy holding HONNECHY outpost 12.00. Kept Cavalry column towards that place. Attacked again N.W. of HONNECHY about 15.30 hrs against Hostile Batty & MGs. Lieut. A.A. BONTOR wounded while with 3rd Dragoon Guards. Batty again advanced to close up to rearmost of Foot 3rd D.G. Regiment and came under heavy shell & rifle crossing railway, but carried with one horse killed. Reached Brigade area after dark. Shells fell in vicinity of Batty during night. Casualties. Men wounded. | |
| | 10th | 05.00 hrs | March 05.00 to valley E.F. TROISVILLES & the Bois Mauvais. Concentrated till 15.00 hrs. Batty went into action with remainder of 4th Horse R.H.A. over R.C.H.A. Bde about East of LA SOTIERE to shoot Barrage E of NEUVILLY in cooperation with an attack by V Corps. Battery came under heavy shell fire (about 1 hour R.H.A. and 1 officer (Lieut. B. MACLACHLAN R.F.A. attached to this Bde) and 4 then wounded. 14 wheels had also heavily damaged and 3 shells and Eq. wagon lost Horse killed. | |

# WAR DIARY
## or
## INTELLIGENCE SUMMARY.

(Erase heading not required.)

Army Form C. 2118.

"C" Battery, RHA

OCTOBER 1915 III.

| Place | Date | Hour | Summary of Events and Information | Remarks and references to Appendices |
|---|---|---|---|---|
| | 10th | About 19.00 | Battery came out of action and joined 6th Cav Bde in Bivouac at MONTIGNY. | |
| | 11th | | Moved with 6th Cav Bde to ELINCOURT very comfortable billets for men and horses. | |
| | 12th | | Remained ELINCOURT. | |
| | 13th | | Moved to BANTEUX. Bivouac. | |
| | 14th | | Moved to ETRICOURT. | |
| | 15th 16th 17th 18th | | ETRICOURT. | |
| | 19th | | Bde field Day towards VILLERS AU FLOS. | |
| | 20th 21st | | ETRICOURT | |
| | 22 | | Bde Field Day | |
| | 23 to 31st | | Battery moved to larger area at EQUANCOURT. Very comfortable camp. Remained EQUANCOURT. took part in Bde Field Days and continued training. | |
| | | | 2 Lt. G. MURDOCH R.F.A. joined from England during month. | |

J. Hogan Bt Lt. O.C. "C" Bty RHA

# WAR DIARY
## INTELLIGENCE SUMMARY.

"C" Battery RHA

NOVEMBER 1918

| Place | Date | Hour | Summary of Events and Information | Remarks and references to Appendices |
|---|---|---|---|---|
| EQUANCOURT | 1st and 2nd | | Battery took part in Bde Tactical Scheme. | |
| | 3rd | | Bge Tactical Scheme. | |
| | 4th | | Battery celebrated 125th Anniversary. Sports & Concert. | |
| | 5th | | Put on 2¾ hrs notice to move at 15.00 hrs. | |
| | 6th | | Moved to SAINS LES MARQUION. very wet. | |
| | 7th | | Moved to ESQUERCHON, near DOUAI. Billeted in the German huts. | |
| | 8th | | Moved to PERONNE. All horses under cover. | |
| | 9th | | Remained PERONNE. "K" Bty RHA joined 6th Cav Bde as 7th Cav Bde were sent forward independently. | |
| | 10th | | Moved 08.00 hrs with advance Billets at BACHY. These orders cancelled on march & Battery Billeted at VAULX LES TOURNAI. | |
| | 11th | | Moved at 07.00 hrs & took part in operations towards ENGHIEN. Halted just WEST of LEUZE (Centre Section had gone forward with 1st RD) & regard ordered 10.30 that Cease Fire" would sound at 11.00 hours, Armistice having been signed. Excitement terrific. All officers of Brigade paraded in Square of LEUZE & at 11.00 hrs hymn "Te Deum" was sounded "Cease fire" Infantry band played "God Save the King" etc. Rear Bde impromptu Yamaska. Copy of Message received from Cavalry Corps at 10.00 hrs "Hostilities will cease at 11.00 to day Nov 11. Troops will stand fast on line reached at hour named aaa Line of outposts will be established and reported to Cav Corps aaa Remainder of troops will be collected and organised ready to meet any demand aaa All military precautions will be pursued and there will be no communication with the enemy aaa Further instructions will be issued aaa Acknowledge. From Cav Corps 08.10." Battery moved back to VAULX LES TOURNAI. Everyone very tired & very tired. | |

S. Nutt. Major RHA

Army Form C. 2118.

# WAR DIARY
## or
## INTELLIGENCE SUMMARY.
(Erase heading not required.)

"C" Battery R.H.A.      NOVEMBER 1918 (Cont)

| Place | Date | Hour | Summary of Events and Information | Remarks and references to Appendices |
|---|---|---|---|---|
| WASMES | 12. | | Moved to billets in WASMES | |
| | 13. | | All ranks busy polishing harness, burnishing steel work etc ready to march to RHINE. | (Arty Tournai 105,000) |
| | 16. | | | |
| | 17. | | Started 07:30 & marched to billets in THORICOURT. 26 miles trying road. | |
| | 18. | | Marched 08:00 to billets in HAUT FRANTISE – RUE HAUTE & GENETTE. 12 miles. Marched in splendidly. Villages decorated with flags etc. Great enthusiasm of people. | |
| | 19. | | Same billets. | |
| | 20. | | | |
| | 21. | | Marched with Brigade 08:15 hours. Got to div. WATERLOO at 12 noon. First British Battery thro'. Great reception in way at BRAINE L'ALLEUD. Local band played all sorts of tunes. Billeted in CEROUX MOUSTY. Very cold. | |
| | 22. | | Marched 08:00 hrs to billets in NOVILLE SUR MEHAIGNE | |
| | 23. | | Same billets. Here had 3rd Cav Bde HQ mess guard. Everyone very disappointed. | |
| | 24. | | Moved to billets in WARISOULX | |
| WARISOULX | 25. | | | |
| | 30. | | Still same billets. Canadian Infantry passing through moving EAST. | |

D. Sutt
Major RHA
Cmdg. "C" Battery RHA.

www.ingramcontent.com/pod-product-compliance
Lightning Source LLC
Chambersburg PA
CBHW081242170426
43191CB00034B/2009